To Lorraine, fellow poet.
Love,

Ben Nuttall-Smith

A
MOMENT
IN
ETERNITY

Other Books by Ben Nuttall-Smith

Blood, Feathers and Holy Men – Historical Novel (Libros Libertad 2011)

Secrets Kept / Secrets Told – Novel/Memoir (Libros Libertad 2012)

Henry Hamster Esquire – an illustrated story for children. (Nuttall-Smith 2012)

Grandpa's Homestead – Haiku for children of all ages, illustrated by Jan Albertin. (Nuttall-Smith 2012)

Postcards (Silver Bow Publishing 2013)

A MOMENT IN ETERNITY

Copyright © 2013 Silver Bow Publishing
Box 5 – 720 – 6th Street,
New Westminster, BC
V3C 3C5   CANADA

Copyright © 2013 Silver Bow Publishing

Cover Photo/Art: Ben Nuttall-Smith
Cover Design: Janet Kvammen
Layout & Design: Candice James
Editing: Candice James

All rights reserved including the right to reproduce or translate this book or any portions thereof, in any form

Library and Archives Canada Cataloguing in Publication

First Edition

ISBN 978-1-927616-02-4

silverbowpublishing@gmail.com
© 2013 Silver Bow Publishing
ISBN 978-1-927616-02-4

Silver Bow Publishing
Box 5 - 720 Sixth St.,
New Westminster, BC
V3L 3C5 CANADA
Email: silverbowpublishing@gmail.com

Website: http://silverbowpublishing.shawwebspace.ca

Table of Contents

Nature   9

Summer Storm
Footpath To The Sea
Lament
Slipper Game
Crescent Beach Reflections
She
A Walk In The Woods In October
Night Falls
Penny's Garden
Ocean Dock on Gambier Island
Deer In The Garden
Maple Leaf
The Fly
Butterfly Wings
Sugar Time
This Beach
Fisherman's Lament
Sechelt Summer
You Don't Know Snow
Winter Preferences

Friends and Lovers   25

Terpsichore
Without Your Love
Rhoda
Handyman's Delight
To Jimmy Paul
Winter
Ode to Mother
Let's Begin
Beach Meditation
Desire

Of Places and People   35

Homeless
Granville Street
The Telephone
A Father's Prayer

Almost Retired
Mother
Mother's Gift
Moon Message
The Artist I Know
When You Make Music
Quand Tu Fais La Musique
New Poetry
The Kiss, The Moment, The Jar
Hospital Window
Fix
Via Rail
Nursing Home
The Appointment
Vancouver
West Coast Morning
Granville Island Reflection
Bar Room Ballad
Idyll Invaded
Bottled Water
Irreverence of Chatter
Christmas Wish List
The Major
Childhood Memories
Nolite Timere
The Public Library

Haiku   59

War and Violence   65

The Old Man
The Bomb
Chelsea Terrors
A Poem for Gaza
Angel of Freedom
Time
Blue
Overheated Planet
Crusaders of the New Tomorrow
Through Music - Peace
Were I Made King of the World
My World

Songs of Birth   77

Tiny Speck
Here I Come
A Moment In Eternity
Arise, My Muse!

Parody & Nonsense   83

Mother Goose
Hey, Dude!
Where's My Wallet?
Sonnet To Travel
Cathedral Cat
Sam
Adam and Eve
Me and My Cat
Self Portrait
Hospital Room
Old Lady in the Sea

Children   93

Mischievous Teddy
Shopping
A Day At The Zoo
Ghostly Moon
Fairy Circle
Night Light
Sticky Finger Marks
Tantrum Tycoon
Billy's Bullfrog
Billy's Bicycle
Wiggly Fingers

* **AUTHOR PROFILE**   *Inside Back Cover*

Nature

SUMMER STORM

summer storm strikes.
tumbling,
sky-black giants trespass.
soggy,
sun slips out of sight.
cymbals clash,
heavens' floodgates open.
rain pummels the pond.
lily pods hunker down tight on the water.

swallow dips
under crown of rose bush.
safe and secure
beneath her majesty.

shaken rose,
drips pink teardrops.
sky-black giants dissolve.
soggy sun emerges triumphant.
summer storm subsides.

FOOTPATH TO THE SEA

with aching limbs and gnarled, knobby cane
the old man puffs, pants to keep astride
his youthful companions cantering down
the winding footpath to the sea.
he arrives, he sits, his gasping abates.

children race, shout with joy to reach the cove;
chase gulls, from congregation on the slip of splintered shell
among the frothy weed and stones,
to frantic flight.

the old man sits in silence, watches, remembers.
a tear slides down his cheek.

LAMENT

one day,
when forests are mountains of rock,
when rivers and streams are deserts of sand,
the air will turn grey
and the sky will be black.
the world will be gone
with no chance to turn back.

monuments will be meaningless
with no one to see them.
the great play will be over,
the theatre empty.

and will you be content
when all life is gone,
when the great cities tumble
and there breaks no new dawn?

so verily now I say unto you
to thwart this fate, here's what you must do:

give up your fortunes,
sow seeds to the fields.
don't let greed take charge.
she sows bitter yields.
when you hear someone crying
bring them in from the cold.
let no child go hungry.
share your knowledge and gold.

His legacy misspent
is God's greatest lament.

SLIPPER GAME

i sit snugly,
cozy in comfy slippers,
teasing the cat
with soft playful kicks.

with fierce concentration
and swish of tail
he pounces and nips,
pounces and nips.

my slippers…
they are the prey.
he is the hunter

I slip out of my slippers.
the game continues.
the pussy puts paw
where toes have vacated;
swatting, tossing,
pouncing,
attacking the slippers
'til they rip and tear.

my slippers,
torn and tattered,
victims of a feline game
and,
my relentless teasing.

CRESCENT BEACH REFLECTIONS

Great expanse of mud and sand,
a rocky bank and water birds,
joggers in the rain.
Brown ever turns to brilliant gold,
when sunshine dapples through the clouds,
to paint the trees with silver lace
and sparkle on the bay.
A stately conference of Heron
debate the gulls about the evening catch
and call the tide to shore.
Above the mottled pools, a pair of eagles glide
while crows protest the rumbly train
that groans and grinds its way
around the headland to the bay.
In early May, the children flock like ducklings,
with buckets and spades, boots and yellow hats.
They squat in puddles, tease the crabs,
and dig for oceans in the watery sand.
Along the shore, their minders sit on logs.
While they watch, they chatter, drink their tea,
and call in vain to stragglers in the pools.
As far as the eye can see, the paddlers wander out
on miles and miles of sand and weed, through shallow pools,
all shimmering beneath the morning glare.
Gulls, white, brown, grey, squabble at a hamper
in the sand, while wrappers gaily flutter in the wind.
A dozen kites swim hard against the breeze,
like minnows with long waggling tails.
One swoops to chase a crow; and then its crosspiece snaps,
to meet stern justice on the rocks below.
Despite the angry stones hurled at its taunts,
the crow flaps down to strut and sound rebuke.
With blankets, chairs, umbrella, hamper, radio,
another gang of picnickers arrives by car,
to taste a summer day at Crescent Beach.
Through steamy miles of traffic horns and roaring trucks,
they've traveled far, to sit upon the sand
and blare their choice of joy for all to share.

SHE

Hulls of orange, purple, banana yellow, lime green;
striped sails billowing and pulling, the sailboats glide,
like quetzal feathers on aquamarine glass.

The froth and spume wash over my feet.
I stand,
a stranger on the shore,
silent, serene.

She emerges
from the sea green water world,
with a slow, sultry, diaphanous rhythm,
dripping translucent diamonds.

She smiles,
emerald eyes emblazoned,
hypnotizing me once again.

Beaded and sun-kissed,
her abalone earrings sparkle.
necklace of snowy pearl gleaming,
her damp silver hair glistens
under the hot tropical sun,

She is
warmer than the sand and sea.

She is
my love,
my destiny.

A WALK IN THE WOODS IN OCTOBER

Nature nudges the season's breast,
into a million subtle hues,
spreading her technicolour mantle
brighter than Joseph's fabled coat.

We stroll through October's perfume,
in the palm of a forest citadel,
embraced by the hush of leaves falling.

The burnt amber sky vibrates,
in ghostly whispers and sighs,
setting the table for twilight.
Nature nudges our hearts,
as we walk inside her harmony
through these October woods.

NIGHT FALLS

Teardrops fall from the trees.
Moonlight sweeps pathways
through the broken clouds.
Night falls and shawls the shore.

Bats flit for fireflies on the bay.
A lonely loon calls.
A twig snaps in the dark.
Something moves behind me. Not real.
Ghostly, hazing in and out.

Night falls apart in surreal pieces
Breaking the dawn to the day.

PENNY'S GARDEN

A wild garden grows
by a cottage near the bay.
The trellis is old and faded
but beauty still climbs her frame,
and crowns the posts
where the garden gate was hung.

Thick moss beneath the cypress tree
stretches onto the old rope swing.
Periwinkle scatters on the garden path
where Thrushes still warble and sing.

The clematis reaches tall
to the bickering blackbirds
protesting the mere presence
of an old yellow cat
perched on the great stone wall.

This is Penny's garden,
and perhaps it's known better days
but old memories survive and come alive
when I walk that Periwinkle path
at dusk with Penny's ghost.

OCEAN DOCK ON GAMBIER ISLAND

Crystal waters, cold and clear,
windowing the secret life of shellfish, starfish and crabs
hopscotching over briny rocks
beneath the urchin-hugged pier.

Mist droplets sprinkle
the essence of fresh pine and iodine.
Birdsong, water swish and dock sounds massage the ear
grinding out a majestic rhythm,
the heartbeat of Gambier Island.

DEER IN THE GARDEN

summer sun not too high,
deer in my garden,
sheer beauty for beauty's sake,
maneuvering deftly through the rows
sampling this and that.

they choose to linger longest,
over the raspberries,
nature displaying a sweet tooth.
they chew them, savour them
til the juice runs in rivers
staining their lips red.

they take their leave
dressed in satisfaction,
lipstick and fur.
The garden party is over.

MAPLE LEAF

Fair Maple, standing stately
in the glistening snows;
tall and lofty sentinel,
your bright red leaf,
the mark of freedom, unfurls patriotically
on our pristine flag of white,

A shape, an emblem
known far and wide;
the sovereign stamp of freedom,
you stand for Canada. You stand for us.

When Spring rain melts the snow
and silver fades to green
your emblem will remain
Shouting, for all to hear, freedom's name.

THE FLY

The swatter moves
Like a slow motion rumbling train
toward the fly.
With ample time
to contemplate
another taste
before flight,
the fly feasts at his leisure.
What is our instant
to the insect whose span of life
is but a moment in the sun?

What is a Universal instant
When our span of life
is only a fleeting glint
in its starry eyes?

BUTTERFLY WINGS

Do you hear
butterfly wings
above the breeze

voices
bird song
dogs barking
cats purring
melodies playing
babies crying
children laughing
old man coughing

sounds
lapping waves
footsteps
door slamming
motor scooter

Hush…
you'll hear
butterfly wings

SUGAR TIME

In springtime, when the thaw winds
Bring the sugar farmer home,
I will hurry to the bush land,
Near my place by Saint Jerome.

Light the fires and scrub the cauldrons.
Tap the maples' steady flow.
Busy friends take time to join me,
Making taffy in the snow
Near my place by Saint Jerome.

THIS BEACH

Sitting on driftwood,
Alone but not lonely,
I gaze at the moon
As it rubs its knuckles
Over the sand
And shines this beach to silver.

Twilight flexes her fingers
Opening up the night.
A sparkle of stars
Arouses an ebony sky

On this beach tonight,
Waves, undulate, splash,
Making love in ethereal grace
To the craggy shore.

As the weary waves ebb
They etch fading initials
Onto the wet obsidian rock
Leaving behind no trace
Of their eternal triumph.

Silence invades on little mouse feet.

Alone, but not lonely,
I continue to gaze at the moon.

There have been many nights,
Magnificent nights,
Glorious, majestic nights,
But none as spectacular
As this night
On this beach.

FISHERMAN'S LAMENT

Our boat's at the dock
With the nets all put by.
We have to wait.
The source is now dry.
The Cod and the Salmon,
Heading to spawn,
Will be pulled from the ocean
Ere the season is done.

The rights of our fathers,
And fathers before,
Have been given away.
We'll be fishing no more.
My heart's with the ocean.
My skill's in the sea.
The waves and their motion
Keep calling to me.

I'm sick of the dole, boys;
I just want to fish.
It's all the same old noise.
No one gets their wish.
If I were a wizard
I'd change things a'right;
Then we'd be fishing
By day and by night.

But I'm just a working man
Who's got work no more,
And it's hard to maneuver
My sea legs on shore.
So I live by the ocean
And I sleep in a tent,
And moan to the moon
My fisherman's lament.

SECHELT SUMMER

on a sunny Sunday afternoon,
dreams sway on silent breezes,
diamonds dance on sparkling seas.

sailboats slap on unbreakable glass.
sleek seals bob through its gloss surface;
small black specks
appearing
and disappearing
in rippling wakes.

moody waves
caress and crash
the stony shores of islets,
frothing at the mouth.

summer wearies
of chasing the wind,
lies down to rest,
falls asleep,
on a grass covered hill
in the heart of West Sechelt.

YOU DON'T KNOW SNOW

You don't know snow
until you've heard coyotes howl;
your eyes and whiskers frosted shut
and from your nether regions, feeling gone.
If hell is real, there'll be no fire
just icy winds across a barren plain.

You don't know snow
until the saw-edged bite of frost
burns your numbed toes and fingertips
when they're forced awake.

WINTER PREFERENCES

You dream of a white Christmas
with icy winds and snow,
and carolers dressed up like bears
at thirty-six below.

I dream of a palm tree beach,
a warm sun in the sky,
a good book, a tall glass,
and a sweetheart at my side.

I don't have the legs to ski.
ice-hockey's not my thing.
I'd rather fly South to the sun
than be North wintering.

There's different strokes for different folks
And when all's said and done.
You stay here with your snow and ice
And I'll have fun in the sun.

Friends

and

Lovers

TERPSICHORE

last night,
Terpsichore,
my princess
fluttered white silk,
pulsed moonbeams,
incandescent
in her beauty.

her halo stayed my heart
and took away my breath.

we danced
in gentle rhythm,

father and daughter
in ritual parting.

a little girl,
bride to handsome consort.

a grown man,
tears in his eyes,
for the things
that won't come again.

WITHOUT YOUR LOVE

Gentle hand on neck and back,
so much love in that touch.
Your fingers bring peace, a soothing balm.
No word needed, your caress says all.

You rekindle my fire as the flame sputters low.
You're my strength when vigour seems lost.
My inspiration, my heart and soul,
You are -- my life.

RHODA

puddles
splashing,
white boots in the rain.
you're beside me .
your hand on my shoulder.
you look down
as i look up.
now
i kiss your tiny hands…
memories of childhood.

you are gone,
yet,
forever here.
you threw candies to the children,
fed me hot rum and lemon.
i slept in your arms.

you loved me.
oh, how i loved you…
love you still.

HANDYMAN'S DELIGHT

i *chose* to live high on that hill
above the ocean, in that tiny house
that needed so much care
top to bottom,
where rats sat glaring
from basement corners.

they ran across my bed at night
and tickled with their whiskers
while i tried in vain to sleep
to the cough and sputter and squeak
of the oil furnace reek,
while centipedes and spiders
crawled across my pillow in the dark.

smoky rays of morning sun
peeped through the rickety blind
that hung by a thread,
over the sliding glass doors
that led to the patio with cracked cement.

ants marched single file,
in snaking columns,
under the door to the Coca Cola can
that sat in front of the dusty brick fireplace
full of soggy newspapers
and rusty tins.

all that
was far better
than natter, natter, natter.

TO JIMMY PAUL

they was callin' guys up.
i'm as good as the rest.
i'm a Shíshálh.
proud Canadian too,
ready to fight for king and country.
Red Ensign flag,
my country ,
my nation ,
so i go.
wear the tartan and the rifle
and march to Sicily in worn-out boots.
in Germany
this kraut shoots through
my hand and my arm.

still got three good fingers.
still can shoot a rifle
and lift a pint
or two,
or three,
but
i can't lift a pint
when i ain't allowed in;
then they kick me off the reserve
and say
you not status indian,
an' people look at me and say
hey, Jimmy Paul, where the hell ya bin?

hell of a lot they know.
government kept my pension too,
most of it anyway.
hell, yes, i love my country.
do it all again.
god damn Ottawa!
let me buy you a beer.
this one's on me.

WINTER

this haunt of freshest nature,
now barren and desolate since you and i
last stood here as one.
orchards and fields bewail their widowed state,
stripped of their brood.

ah! what fond memories this spot brings back:,
glorious, intimate times:
your smiles,
your tears,
forgiveness for a lovers' spat.
two hearts melting to one.

but, just as autumn's cold, cruel winds
strip gentle nature to the bone,
insensitive death descended on the wings of time
to carry you away
and leave me here…alone.

ODE TO MOTHER

Where are you now, mother?
In that great realm of nothingness and everything;
of all that's past and all that's still to be?

Who are you now, mother?
Did all those absolutes you knew as truth
help you to find forgiveness for your doubts?
And after all the turmoil of your life,
are you at peace at last?

Will I recognize your spirit,
if on some distant sphere we chance to meet?
Or will we pass as ghosts by night,
and miss each other in our search,
Evangelines upon some misty shore?

LET'S BEGIN

Had I my life to live again
and knew what I know now,
I'd do a few things differently:

I'd guard my tongue from hurtful words
no matter how provoked.

I'd save more for a rainy day.
spend less on wasteful toys.

I'd try to help a neighbour in his need;
not seeking to be known
but giving from the heart.

I'd be a better lover;
not looking to be loved
but desiring to give love.

I'd be the kind of dad I wish I'd had.
forever gentle,
listening all the time.

Had I my life to live again,
how different things would be
but Nature does not chew her cabbage twice.

I only have these fading moments
left to share with you.

Better late than never,
I begin.

BEACH MEDITATION

i stand on the tidal verge,
face the open sea.
conscious of my breath
i breathe in deeply,
and feel the ocean swell inside me.

i join my hands together,
clasped loosely;
stretch arms over head, left, right;
exhale, inhale,
more conscious of my breathing.

Slowly bend my knees,
squat to touch my heels;
inhale, exhale,
i am becoming my breath.

i rise.
position my body to face the sun,
assume the lotus position,
relax, close my eyes;
exhale, inhale,
my body lightens, floats away.
i am my breath.

i contemplate the waves,
brackish and inviting,
until I am the waves.
I smell the morning breeze,
filled with ocean scent,
filled with me.
I become the breeze.

Inhale, exhale,
breathing more shallow now.
body loses weightlessness.
I return to myself,
beach meditation over.

DESIRE

You thought I was dead when you came near.
In silken negligée, your body beckoned.
I felt your pulse.
I felt the yearning of your youth
My loins ached to celebrate your beauty,
To caress your slim, firm body.

I did not disclose my craving.
My heart throbbing, I did not cry out,
"Love me! Love me! Love me!"

An old building still holds warmth.
There's still fire in the furnace.
Recalling the taste of whiskey wet kisses
Teases my soul,
Awakens my body.

I am not dead.
My heart knows love.
My soul knows fire.
I know desire.
I glow, spark,
burst into hottest flame.

The embers are not dead.

Of Places and People

HOMELESS

She spends her long days
curled up on tattered rags
and soggy cardboard mats,
in crooked doorways
and by graffiti marked dumpsters,
on the cold hard sidewalk,
drowning slowly in the unforgiving rain.
When she's hungry
she roots for scraps of second hand, spoiled food,
behind greasy spoons and burger joints,
dining in bleak alleys on dark side of skid row.

Should she chance to find a half-inch butt
that's not been crushed,
she'll cadge a light,
remembering when she smoked a pack a day.
Those days long gone now,
just a hazy memory.

Once, she went to work each morning,
drove her kids to daycare and school.
For nineteen years she worked;
then, one day, she walked away.
No one knew where she'd gone
or why.

Now here she is,
a broken down angel,
a tarnished woman
wrapped in tattered rags
and shattered dreams.

With fixed stares,
we all hurry by her.
We don't even want to know
her name.

GRANVILLE STREET

breathless,
pacing fast
past theatres,
book stores,
assorted junk.

punk is in:
purple hair,
spiked,
tattooed torsos,
pierced
lips, tongues, ears.

despair:
crouched,
slouched,
hands extended.

pretend not to see
hurry, hurry, hurry,
look straight ahead.
dread the reeling drunk
avoid.
paranoid,
hold tight to wallet and keys.

"please, my baby's starving
just a quarter.
daughter needs milk"
smell of booze.
who's in charge of so much misery?
misery.
misery.
been there too,
but
not as deep
as she.

THE TELEPHONE

She wanders in and out of dreams,
on the bustling city sidewalk,
just outside the big box store,
in a daze,
in a haze.
There's a package in her hand;
what it is she can't recall.

She holds a cellphone, wrapped in plastic,
wrapped in plastic, wrapped in plastic.
Her ears ring.
"The telephone!
It has my number!
Ring! Ring! Ring! Ring!
Can't get in! Can't get in!"

Someone taps her on the shoulder:
"'Scuse me, ma'am. Please come with me."
"Just a moment, sir," she mumbles.
"Can't you hear?
My phone is ringing. Phone is ringing.
But, oh God! I can't get in.
Can't get out. Can't get out."

Shoppers, children stop to stare.
All around they stare, and laugh,
push and grab, push and grab.
Still, the telephone is ringing.
Phone is ringing. Phone is ringing.
Her head spinning,
spinning, spinning, spinning, spinning.

"Hello? Hello? Hello? Hello?"
She wanders in and out of dreams
In a haze,
In a daze

A FATHER'S PRAYER

Let me be loved even more than respected,
and respected more than admired.
May I be wanted for myself alone
and not for the gifts I bring.

In what I say, let me be wise;
let me not offend with careless slips.
Forgive the foibles of my youth.
and the fury of my middle years.

Most of all, let me hold my tongue
when my counsel is not asked for.

ALMOST RETIRED

He puffs and sweats the steep incline
to the cabin door,
head drooped, he drags each step
then stops, to catch his wind.

So much to live for now,
beyond the daily grind.
He toiled to earn his rest
not knowing when to stop the race.
He puffs and sweats, can't catch his wind.
at the cabin door,
he is gone.

MOTHER

The years have traced their splendor on your brow.
Sweet souvenirs of your faithful toil.
Don't hide your silver strands.
They match your heart of gold.
Each passing year's a tribute to your grace.
Your smiles, forever etched into our hearts;
The tears you shed have now become a rose.

MOTHER'S GIFT

Mother gave the gift of spoken word,
a love of poetry and comic song,
from childhood horsey rides to A.A. Milne,
peppered with the haunting tales of Poe.

Then,
William Shakespeare's *Sonnets,*
William Johnson's *Sermons,*
The *Adventures* of R. L Stevenson,
and Robert Service tramping through the drifts.

The drama placed on every phrase;
The joy her voice imparted
are etched forevermore into my soul.

The echoes of my childhood –
Mother's gifts.

MOON MESSAGE

I whispered your name to the moon
on a stained glass night
filled with starspun madness.
Did she tell you?

I searched the streets of the town,
the beaches, parks and tides
trying to find you.

A fog shrouded down,
hiding my eyes,
hiding my tears,
hiding the moon.

At that moment, I realized…
She'd never tell you.

THE ARTIST I KNOW

I paint a picture
to remind me of you.
I shade it with white marble shadows
the essence of wind-blown trees.
I paint regal banks of ocean bluff
with waves crashing, breaking,
kneeling in reverence at their base;
A harsh invitation
To a tender tryst.

There is movement.
Living strokes, the texture of tears,
where shaggy brown dogs lie down
by park-benched men,
lost in their own splash of splendour.

There are boys standing, glossy and tanned,
in boats with billowing sails.
Each face has a story to tell.

I brush clowns and children
into the painting,
wearing top hats and tap shoes,
riding horses and eagles
through diamond horizons.

I paint a tale of epic proportion,
overflowing with pomp and glory,
onto a ribbon of sacred rainbow
to remind me of you…
an artist filled with love.

WHEN YOU MAKE MUSIC

your fingers
tease,
tingle,
vibrate,
caress,
and flutter like a butterfly.

memories swirl
in a potpourri of
lullaby,
waltz,
pavane,
prelude.

i rise, anew
in love
with music,
with you.

QUAND TU FAIS LA MUSIQUE

vos doigts taquinent le clavier
picotent mon oreille
vibrent mon esprit
remuent mon âme
caressent

et mon coeur
oscille comme un papillon
avec les vagues de mémoires tourbillées
de prélude
de pavane
de valse
de berceuse
et la vie est renouvlée
en amour
avec la musique
et avec toi

NEW POETRY

you stepped into my life.
new atmosphere
filled
with rhapsodies.

you smiled.
the sun escaped its shroud
threw off its shackles.

your kiss
was new life.

you touched my heart.
I became new poetry.

THE KISS, THE MOMENT, THE JAR

silver hair, not grey,
shining like Chinese silk
emblazoned with butterflies.

earrings, white shell,
glistening, dangling,
whispering in your ear.

turquiose sweater,
warm, hugging your breasts,
satisfied, contented.

book on your lap
speaking to you.

you look up. see me watching you,
blow me a kiss.
i catch the kiss, and the moment,
keep them in a jar in my mind…
a safe place to hide in harder times.

HOSPITAL WINDOW

outside my hospital window
a gun metal grey sky threatens,
amid a backdrop of roaring, whining
trucks, cars and ambulances.

i lie alone,
half here, half gone.
hanging on…
just another way of living.
marking time.

i lie asleep-awake;
listening to distant voices
i can't quite hear;
envisioning distant horizons
i can't quite see;
dreaming distant dreams
i can't quite fathom.

as the distance closes in
with choke hold certainty
reality shrinks, fades.

outside my window,
a silent sky
and i.

FIX

He's dying in his alcohol-tobacco breath,
drug shot eyes cockroach infested room,
stained walls, newspaper-pasted windows,
despair and sweat, anger and tears.
nowhere to go.
busted, needs a fix.
broken, can't be fixed.

VIA RAIL

clickety-clack.
railroad track.
rattle and shake
bump of the wheels
train clips along
moaning,
groaning,
through flashpoint green
of forest glade.
crossing gates
clanging loudly
resonance fades
as "g" force expands

kaleidoscope sky,
burnt ochre fields,
waterfalls washing
mountain faces,
barnyards and farmhouses
silos and sheds
glinting red
gleaming yellow
under a scorching sun

backcountry delicacy
via rail's exclusive menu
filling the eye
engraving the mind
satisfying the soul

NURSING HOME

forced into radical reassessment:
life gallops by,
a sequence of nows;
days drag on,
a series of hours.

empty halls and dusty rooms:
shuffling slippers,
stagnant smell of sweat and urine.

like a monk, he sips in silent hisses,
toothless, tasteless.
he dribbles on whiskered chin and gown

he sleeps in drug induced tranquility,
with lost independence
and thwarted sexuality.

the clock ticks down,
ticks down,
ticks down.
soon…
he'll be gone with the wind.

THE APPOINTMENT

I feel pretty good. I'm up for the struggle:
Friday in the city.
angry traffic crawls, stops, crawls.
At last, I find a parking space,
coin the meter,
run three blocks to the clinic.
Late, always late.

In the waiting room,
I wait with waning patience and
dour-faced matrons,
phlegmy coughs,
squalling kids with runny noses.

The clock ticks.
The parking meter, out of earshot,
must be clicking.

Still I wait – and fidget.
I toy with a magazine,
last year's copy, pages missing.

I grab a coin from my change purse,
tell the nurse I'll be right back,
run hard to the meter.
Damn! Too late! Expired.
unwelcome, dog-eared ticket on my windshield.

I leave the ticket in plain view.
The hungry meter's had its meal.
I run back to the clinic.
The nurse summons me to the desk.
"The Doctor was called away
on an emergency while you were gone.
We'll have to reschedule your appointment."

Friday city traffic, parking ticket, wallet lighter....
Now, I do feel sick.

VANCOUVER

we cycle on paths where the grass is green
below snow - covered peaks in april sun
boats in the harbour, bobbing at anchor
rippling reflections of tall buildings
clean-vibrant-oriental-western
cherry blossomed avenues
dogwood   daffodil
totems   tulips
rhododendron
city in bloom
**
*

WEST COAST MORNING

Dawn haze lifts from turquoise, beige,
radiant edifice – fifteen shades
green and blue;
smudge of robin's egg peeking through
to promise sun and maybe sprinkles
here and there;
a pleasant walk
or sea-wall cycle in between.

All about the city – cars, coach, sky-rail
wend their way to shop or school.
Motorists seldom blare or honk.
Lotusland a laid-back burg,
throngs moving, grooving,
happy purpose in their gait;
time to stop for early brew;
recyclers smile as they retrieve
their forenoon treasures.

West coast morning,
sweeping clean,
fulfilled.

GRANVILLE ISLAND REFLECTION

Guitar picker crooning
while two deaf-mutes sign so loud
can't hear the words he's sobbing
into the shaky microphone
under the red awning
on a lazy Granville Island
summer afternoon

Tiny tot
tied to his nanny
by a loving eye
teases pigeons
while midday shoppers hunt for parking spots
and long-haired daddy in sandals and shorts
dripping ice cream cone in one hand,
pushes a stroller with the other.

Give the man a loonie
for the song,
for his sorrow,
to assuage the loneliness.

BAR ROOM BALLAD

Piano player, keyed up, beats steady time.
Patrons shout oblivious to the song, the man;
tipsy lovers swirl about the hang out.
His art is lost in a haze of smoke and mirrors.

Somewhere in the din
a tear-filled lyric touches a patron,
the one with the sad blue eyes.
Recalling the tune, she takes a stranger's hand,
and they dance
to the end of love.

IDYLL INVADED

In her garden by the sea,
she sips coffee with the morning news.
I sit beneath a parasol in the cool shade
with a glass of sweating cold lemonade.

A Hummingbird flits under the fuchsia buds.
A Heron puffs and preens.

Whiffs of tiny cloud ramble
Above the long stretch of damp, grey, sandy spit.
Butterflies and birds flutter and cluster.
Silver wings gleam overhead.
Two boys toss a baseball back and forth
On a lazy summer morning.
A peaceful easy feeling pervades.

Then the sudden change-up:

Freight train whistles by, with chugs and bangs.
Drivers park cars, slam doors.
Rappers and rockers blare on radios,
Screeching tires squeal with delight,
Growling motors threaten with joy.

Beyond the fence, an argument.
The noisy city folk have entered the area,
Bruised the atmosphere,
Killed the serenity.

Idyll invasion complete.

BOTTLED WATER ($2.64)
Downtown Toronto, May 2012

What is life
to the poor
in this big city?
Can we truthfully
call it living?
Can they?

$2.50 can't buy
bottled water.
Fountains
where children drank
freely
are gone.

Rainwater puddles
are coated in oil.
washroom doors
open only
for cash
or plastic privilege.

One day, soon,
fresh air may be sold,
will be sold

You and I
will fade away.

Corporate Sponsors
won't mourn
our passing.

IRREVERENCE OF CHATTER

There's sacrilege in gaudy chatter
within this sacred ground,
while laureates nourish parched souls
with lyric sustenance.

Elegance flowing from a poet's lips.
Weeping at the magnificence of memories,
nectarine words, passion of spirit.

The moment will not last
but the rasping of your irreverence
will scratch my peace, even when I'm gone.

I cannot protest the seaplanes rising from the harbour.
I do not challenge the shouting of crows,
but I do object to your raucous invasion of this sacrosanct space.

I move closer to stand within reach of his voice.
Your screechy chatter follows.
Everything is sacrilege.

I cringe at your ignorance.
I weep for the laureates
I sigh at my inability to stop
your constantly moving mouth
from spewing
this incessant stream
of irreverent chatter.

CHRISTMAS WISH LIST

My cat and I have hung up our stockings,
We've both been good. Of this I am sure.

Our wish list is short:

Bring peace to the world
warm clothes for the poor,
good food for the starving souls.
Shelter the homeless,
comfort the sick,
set the innocent prisoners free.

And if you can, Dear Old Saint Nick,
for Christmas, a sprinkling of snow.

THE MAJOR

Head bowed in hands,
Is he wrestling the horrors of the front?
Do monsters haunt his dreams as they do mine?

Later, heading home from Mass,
he says not a word to me but
"Pull your socks up boy. Step like a man."
.
We walk in silence.
I, with awkward teenage fears
He, pulling on a cigarette.

The skinny kid from England
and his stepfather.

CHILDHOOD MEMORIES – ENGLAND

Lullabies, horsey rides, stories read from books,
plasticine, song time, picnics in the woods,
Punch and Judy, dressing up, swinging on the gate,
blackberries, stinging nettles. Wasps!

Peppermint, licorice, sparklers on the tree,
Oranges, fairy circles, first snow on the lawn,
Father Christmas, bunnies, and a Teddy bear for me.
green apples, hairbrush, "Ow!"

Pencils, crayons, snuggling by the fire,
camp fires, sing-songs, swimming in the sea,
red boots, puddles, a fishing pole and hooks,
toy trains, aeroplanes, "Bed!"

Lollypops, wishing wells, gypsies in a field,
elephants, monkey nuts, rolling down a hill,
bunny rabbits, crocodiles, ponies, and a deer,
road blocks, air raids. Pow!

Car rides, rope swings, robins in a nest,
gas masks, blackouts, nights beneath the stairs,
pup tents, parachutes, soldiers in a ditch,
doodlebugs, buzz bomb, Dead!

Lullabies, horsey rides, and stories read from books,

"NOLITE TIMERE"
This story has many beginnings. It's the ending that's elusive.

An old man shakes off his city clothes –
Trilby hat in brown plaid,
knee length Burberry,
gray silk cravat,
blue dress shirt with fraying cuffs,
black braided belt, silver buckle,
alligator moc-toe shoes flecked with mud,
stained white over-the-calf socks, garters,

form-fitting riding breeches,
and tattered long-johns.
He drops a boar skin wallet, Gucci watch, Sony Ericsson cell phone
and an assorted set of keys on a ring
into a large bin labeled "recycling".
Then, from a long rack, he selects a rough woolen robe.
Thus garbed, and with cold bare feet, he walks into the night.

Once upon a lifetime,
eons ago, and far into the future,
as suns blaze then sink into silent black holes.
As other universes sizzle into being,
a monk, servant to a timeless Father God or Mother Goddess,
lives alone on a great arid plain.

One long and dusty day,
when the biting winds chew at his blistered nose
and bluebottle flies sting his festering cheeks,
the monk feels his end draw near
and journeys out into the desert.
He sits in the cooling sand.
He gazes at the immensity of stars.
In these times, they sparkle brilliantly,
even in the noon day sun.
The swirling galaxies swarm in the purple sky
as if some astronomical charwoman has shaken out
her dust mop in the great wind.

I know this is true.
I am that lonely monk.
I am old and my joints ache, even in the dry air.
I lift my withered arms high up;
the stars envelop me.

I float like a wafted dry leaf, up inside the Milky Way.
Down mega light years below, I see the planet Earth.
Faster and faster,
it spins like a moth around its flickering candle star.
Soon it's a speck of sand amid a trillion other worlds.

I watch the Earth I had known evaporate.
It is a dewdrop in the morning sun.
My hand is full of spinning orbs of brilliant light.
Meteors pierce my naked thigh.
Yet I feel no fear.

Long ago, my robe of wool and hemp had floated from my limbs.
Suddenly, I feel a light too bright to bear.
At its centre is a spinning, pulsating sphere.
Sometimes the circle is a great triangle.
Other times, it's a tiny baby.

From the light comes a great wind,
blowing in steadily increasing circles.
Shhhhpheeeeuuuw!
I float inside an enormous, living heart.
I hear the steady rhythm.
"Badoom! Badoom! Badoom!"

A timeless voice calls out to me.
At first, it's loud. Then it's soft.
Next it's a whisper, like a breeze in tall pines.
Then I hear an echoing tongue.

I don't recognize that Voice.
Yet I embrace its invading message:
"Ego sum, nolite timere."

It is I. Fear not.

THE PUBLIC LIBRARY

The Public Library,
the great equalizer.
Young and old,
rich or poor,
scholar or ignoramus,
a mixed potpourri of egos
entering without restriction,
drinking in the knowledge of the ages.

Eyes and minds
feasting on the lore of the ages,
traveling to inaccessible corners of the Globe
with the flip of a page,
the push of a button,
the tap of a key.

questions answered
mountains of books,
stacks of magazines,
rows of computers,
librarians, Sherpas and guides.

The Public Library
lender of knowledge
pillar of the community.
conquerer of ignorance…

The pen *is* mightier than the sword!

HAIKU

CHERRY BLOSSOM

Sidewalks dressed in pink –
perfumed veils for city streets.
Vancouver in spring.

BOOKS

Take a book to bed;
read until you fall asleep.
Wake up fresh and bright.

EARTHQUAKE

Earth shakes, buildings fall.
Cherry blossoms on the waves
beckon sailors home.

POLITICAL DEBATE

On television,
the politicians argued.
I drifted to sleep.

HONEYMOON

Icy sheets of silk:
Warm bodies slide together
through the moonlit night.

APRES-SKI

Snow on distant blue;
gone, the winter holidays.
Work begins anew.

SUNSHINE HOLIDAY

Sand beneath my feet
sunlight on my naked back:
Let this moment last.

BACK TO SCHOOL

Rows of restless youth –
their beach adventures ended:
All slouch at their desks.

HOUSE-HUBBY

Dishes in soapsuds;
hubby's turn to make his mark.
He rolls up his sleeves.

ECHO

Laughter rings like bells
against the granite mountains.
Silver trumpets call.

NIGHT SOUNDS

Barn mouse rubs pink paws;
Spider spins her silver lair;
owl hoots from on high.

RAINDROPS

Splattering of rain:
shards of sound like crystal bells.
Echoes in the night.

NATURE

Spider web sparkles,
radiant in wet moonlight.
Captured barn mouse screams.

APRIL COLOUR

Crowds of daffodils,
splattering the countryside,
spread their golden hue.

MORSE CODE

In nature's Morse Code,
scarlet-breasted woodpecker
taps to find a meal.

THE OLD HOMESTEAD

Ghosts of yesteryear
whisper softly through the cracks,
carried by the breeze.

HEN HOUSE

Bugs are everywhere:
Spiders weave in every crack –
Chickens lay their eggs.

BANTAM CHICKS

Bantam hen flaps by
with her brood of yellow chicks
kicking up the dust.

ABANDONED HOUSE

Rotted roof sags down;
screen door banging never stops.
Weeds grow through the floor.

YEAR OF ABANDONMENT

Swimsuit calendar
hanging from a rusty nail –
nineteen-thirty-one.

MOTH

Grey moth beats its wings
against the dusty window.
I watch 'till it dies.

RACOON

Raccoon rubs his hands
like a hungry alderman.
Cheeky little chap.

GOLDEN BUTTERFLY

Golden butterfly
flutters on the daffodil.
Two black whiskers wave.

War and Violence

THE OLD MAN

clatter! bing! bang! boom!
spring pounds on city sidewalks
skateboards scrape
hot tires squeal
shouts and laughter echo off buildings
basketballs bound against post and fence
dribble past
then back and 'round the old man
lost again
in his past

clatter! bing! bang! boom!
battle screams in the night sky
engines roar
ack-acks pound
shouts and curses blatantly sound
big bombs whistle, the walls resound
shrapnel whines past his head

THE BOMB

where were you
when the bomb dropped
when feet and fingers flew
when torsos and limbs
lay in carnage
where were you?

it seems so very long ago
yet just the other night,
and every night
the glazed eyes stare
to scream into his sleep
and drown his tears upon tears
upon tears

where were you?

CHELSEA TERRORS

In 1941, I left my teddy bear behind.
You smothered all my faerie dreams,
drowned my childhood
in Gold Leaf, London Dry,
and flickering silver screen promises.
You oozed over me,
an albuminous silver streak of spotted slug.
You immersed me in your cobwebs and sour sweat.
Night after night after night,
you drove your poison dart deep, deep, deep –
and no one heard my sobs.

Outside your lair,
the Chelsea world screamed another agony.
Before the moaning sirens ceased,
the shrieking metal fell.
it filled the crumbling streets with flames –
and running,
running,
running.

No place was safe
to hide away.

A POEM FOR GAZA

I knew you as a small boy
Playing dreidel in the sand.
Your father was the Rabbi,
Your Mama my best friend.

We went to school together,
And both sang Khanuka songs.
Our days were warm and happy,
Before a thousand wrongs.

I loved you as a brother
Our homes were heart by heart.
But they built a wall of hatred
To drive us far apart.

One day last week I found you
Lying legless in the sand,
A bullet through your shoulder,
An "AK" in your hand.

I knew you as a small boy
Playing dreidel in the sand.
Your father was the rabbi,
Your Mama my best friend.

ANGEL OF FREEDOM

A door opens
Iran spills out
students, artists, lovers –
green ribbons flutter
Hope arises.
Hands stretch in peace signs
words in the streets
cheers, prayers
Allahu akbar
silent marchers –
a hundred thousand pairs of sneakers.
Thought Troopers
blackshirt bullies,
billy clubs,
shots, blood,
mothers' tears.

The Angel of Freedom is dead.
I see her face – daughter, lover, martyr,
my sister, your sister, our sister.

Trust is dead
too much has been taken –
Revolution Avenue screams.

the door slams shut while children die…
and birds still fly over Tehran

TIME

We sit on the cusp of everlasting now,
a point in space and time.
All around is vastness,
a world in turmoil,
the past forever gone;
tomorrow never is.
No use waiting.

BLUE 1

If I press close to the bars
on my tiny window,
I see a splash of cobalt blue.

Blue:
the color of freedom.
No tree, no shade of green in view.
A bird teases with a flap of wings.

Had I those wings,
I'd fly away
and disappear from this painting.

* * * *

BLUE 2

I press close;
squint my eyes,
and see a splash of indigo blue.

The rest is dull grey:
not the slightest hint of green,
not a single leaf.

The tiny speck on the horizon,
probably a sparrow.
The rest is faded yellow.

In the distance, I hear children playing
– a teasing sound.

Tomorrow,
perhaps a different canvas.

OVERHEATED PLANET

Somalia, Afghanistan,
Iraq, Iran and Pakistan,

Syria and Lebanon,
Israel and Palestine,

Bangladesh, Myanmar,
North Korea and Sudan,

South Africa, Zimbabwe,
Chad, Darfur and South Sudan,

Honduras, Colombia,
Haiti, Cuba, Mexico,

Russia, China and Japan,
Great Britain, France and Germany.

The U.S.A., and Canada,
The Multinational zillionaires.

The atmosphere, the biosphere,
All the oceans of the world,

Mix the whole mess in a pot,
Garnish with a sprig of HOPE,
Pour it out and spread while hot
Then cool it with a pint of CARE.

CRUSADERS OF THE NEW TOMORROW

Jackboots crash on cobble highways, gentle byways.
Where pilgrim, knight, and merchant soles once softly swept,
and high-stepping steeds pranced.
monster tanks flaunt and flare their cursed smoke
as they scratch and screech their rumbling blasphemy.

Twisted crosses, black on red,
jigsaw across shields and pennants.
Ever flowing blood feeds fields of poppies,
acres of brilliant poppies,
worlds of poppies.
Who can staunch it?

In the woods, trees bend and break,
twisted, splintered, ruined.
and from heaven's realm, death-screaming eagles
fling down eggs of destruction.
Cathedrals, castles, mansions, hovels, entire cities
are only smoldering memories.

Moaning shells, pale yellow-green gas,
slowly burning corpses piled helter-skelter:
Dogs sniff about, quarrel in the stench.
The torn ones, young and old, moan unconsoled
while mothers clutch wailing infants and weep.
Others stagger about, helpless.

In this rubble of hatred, death, and curses,
a tiny blossom pushes through the toxic dust,
mute promise of a new day
when children may go once more to pick flowers,
sing of peace,
and plan a better tomorrow.

Now we go forth as knights once strode
to spread this dream to those
who have not dared to dream.
Our children fly the eagles hurling eggs of fire

while leaders push the buttons, shout commands
from sheltered desks in padded cells
where screams cannot be heard.

And other children curse the dark
as we once cursed at those
who came to set us free.
Here in this land
where different poppies grow amidst the sands
we taste the poison milk and tap black gold
while teaching them to love our sweet democracy
and bless our names.
As we kill their children to set them free.

THROUGH MUSIC - PEACE

When People sing,
souls leap past race, creed, dress, and tongue,
to grasp brother, sister, and friend
in multi-colored tones
of joy, hope, and love.

WERE I MADE KING OF THE WORLD

Were I made King of the World,
I'd employ vagrants to sweep the cities clean.
All bottles, cans and scrap paper would be recycled with cash back.
Litterers would be sentenced without argument to pick-up duties.

The worst criminals would be sent to collect
cigarette butts and dog crap.
I'd offer tax incentives to repair old buildings.
Derelicts would be torn down, to rebuild housing for the homeless.

Children would have parks to play in.
No child would be denied an education.
Health care would be free with an emphasis on preventive care.
Public transport would replace private cars in cities.
Rapid rail would run from city to city and urban transit would run
from free park-and-ride stations in every community.

Governments would be elected by the people, not by corporations
and every citizen would be required by law to vote.
Worldwide trade would be free with fair competition to all.
Restorative justice would replace punitive prison terms.

With all this,
a king would be redundant.

I'd retire.

MY WORLD

i want to live in a world
where little birds nest in the trees,
i want to feel the breeze
taste the cool clean air
walk down by the river,
see the moon among the ripples,
count the stars
smell wild flowers
and know all the while i am free.

neighbours would be friendly;
they'd be white and brown and black.
i'd know each one by name
to show i truly care.

i want my children to be happy,
my children's children too.
i need to know they'll laugh and sing
and sometimes cry like me.

we'd fight all wars
around a table in a hall of kindness
with wooden soldiers and lead sailors.
the losers and the winners
would sit down to friendly dinners
where we'd cheer the referee,
a child of nine.

what a world this world would be
where i'd need you and you'd need me
and every one we met would smile
and call us "friend and comrade".
if we hurry, we might make it,
change the world before they break it.
call for unconditional love
and bring the madness to an end.

Songs of Birth

TINY SPECK

when i was a tiny speck
in mother's womb
beneath her beating heart
the jungle drummed

morning sickness
cursing me
loving me
singing to me
savage lullabies

i heard the rhythm
moved

i kicked
to say
I love you

HERE I COME

a primeval fish
swimming softly
in your primordial sea
i visualize
your bed on a silent Sunday morning
when all the world is sleeping
and we are wrapped
together
awake
inside this moment
we knew would come

A MOMENT IN ETERNITY

how beautiful
floating like an astronaut
on your lifeline
listening to starlit lullabies

womb to world
birth unfurled
my grand daughter!

tiny legs push
tiny hands flex

to grasp my fingers;
i lift you up
our eyes meet

a moment in eternity
bonds forged, solidified
i remain
amazed

ARISE, MY MUSE!

My muse lies panting,
drained,
exhausted
I search for words,
to celebrate
my second grandchild,
this gorgeous boy
now tugging at my heart.

I play the jolly fool
to fetch a smile,
drop to all fours,
play peek-a-boo,
dip and banter
to elicit a laugh.

Arise, my muse,
to gallop like a horse beneath the rein.
to ride with flag unfurled an honour bent.
to bless this sacred child
that bears my mark!

Parody

and

Nonsense

WHERE'S MY WALLET?

I reach into my left pants pocket
and feel stark terror.
My wallet that was there before
is not there now!
My stomach sinks.
When did I last ... ?
I search my luggage;
look about in panic mode.
I'm in a knot.
Nothing.

Oh, God! Please, God!
Quick! Phone the restaurant!
"Please, look to see!" ...
"No, I wasn't at a table.
I only stopped to use the restroom – and telephone."
"No wallet here.
You can't blame us." ...
"Oh, come now, sir.
Don't make a fuss."

That's it! That's it!
It's on the bus!
I phone the depot.
Oh, my God! They put me on hold!
My fingertips grow cold.
"Sorry, sir."
My stomach drops to my toes.
"Oh, wait a minute.
Is your name Ben?"

I'm alive again!

MOTHER GOOSE

Jill's Story

That Jack is such a baby
when it comes to fetching water.
He tossed my pretty kitty down the well
then put the blame on Tommy Flynn
because he'd seen us kissing
at Little Boy Blue's haystack picnic in the dell.

He boasted when he told me about kitty
so I bashed him with my bucket.
I'm glad I broke his crown and made him cry.
He only tumbled for effect
in case you didn't hear him
screeching like a blackbird in a pie.

Jack's Rebuttal

My sister Jill is such a fibber
since she became a women's libber.
I didn't drown her pussy cat
or anything as cruel as that;
And that affair with Tommy Flynn
was her idea. I don't blame him.
She'll make a grab for any guy
Georgie Porgie puddin' and pie,
Bobby Shafto, Tommy Snooks,
as long as they're in story books.

And don't you worry about my nob.
I had it patched by old Dame Dob.

HEY DUDE

You wanna be a poet?
Write me some new verse.
Not the same old same old
you've been scribbling
since you first picked up a pen.

Knock my boots off.
Shout from the rafters.
Scream profanities of pain and happiness.
Give me tears and laughter.
Shake my black soul.
Drag me to my feet.

Hey Dude!
Jolt me.
Kick ass!

SONNET TO TRAVEL

Each time I pack my bags to go abroad,
All seven pairs of socks are picked with care.
My six best shirts, all ironed and neatly stored,
With handkerchiefs, and matching underwear.

I always bring two jerseys, one a spare.
Sometimes those tropic nights can turn quite cool.
And naturally, I'll take my favourite pair
Of jackets, without which I'd look the fool.

For formal evenings, tuxes are the rule.
We ought to be prepared to dine and dance.
My swimming trunks, for lounging by the pool
And, goodness me, let's not forget my pants.

Our destination's picked, we've spared no cost,
We pray this time our bags will not get lost.

CATHEDRAL CAT

my cat's gone away to sing in the choir
at a cathedral by the Black Sea.
i didn't know he was planning to go,
'til he made his announcement at tea.

he packed his pyjamas and toothbrush and comb,
and gave me a hug at the gate.
i whispered "goodbye", with a tear in my eye,
while he rushed off as though he were late.

i hope he enjoys the incredible noise,
though i've heard they put on quite a show.
still, it's terribly far to the "Aya-so-fya"
where the monks used to sing long ago.

they'll "meow" all night long, their sad pussycat song
then they'll feast on fresh catnip and mice.
while i'll miss the dear cat, i could not hold him back.
so a postcard will have to suffice.

my cat's gone to Turkey to sing in the choir,
and he won't be back home for a while.
but he sends me adventures and stories so fine,
and his anecdotes cause me to smile.

my cat's took a trip to sing in the choir
at a cathedral by the Black Sea.
i didn't know I would miss him so,
but tomorrow he comes home to me.

there'll be catnip for him and cookies for me
as we exchange stories and sip on chai tea.
he'll sing me a song he sang with the choir
and happy so help me will happier be.

SAM

Sam had not washed in forty years,
his ears were filled with sand
and seaweed from the great lagoon
and Brussels sprouts and pears.

And everywhere Sam walked splish-splosh
the seagulls came to gawk
and flash their egos loud and brash
then fertilize the land.

Then one dark night at half-past three
the summer sun called out
and we rejoiced with raucous song
and took a trip to Babylon.

Oh, how I wish that you could see
the happy oysters running
free to climb the yum yum tree and dance.
It's more than I can stand.

ADAM AND EVE

Who had the bright idea
to put those fig leaves
on the *Adam and Eve* picture
in my book?

If I were Adam, I'd protest
and pull those damn leaves off
the page to see and touch
her nipples and caress
that special place upon the page.
And I'd insist
she do the same for me.

ME AND MY CAT

we live on a hill in a big sunny house
and we stay in our house all alone.
just me and my cat
and we do as we like
and we like what we do
in our home.

we go to bed late
and we don't change our socks
and our clothes pile up on the floor.
he don't scream at me
and i don't yell at him
and he won't get upset if i snore.

if i can't eat my greens
and he won't drink his milk
we can still get dessert if we want.
'cause there's no one to say
that it's too late to play
so we can if we like
but we won't.

we might stand in the rain
or just howl at the moon.
we don't wear our boots or a hat.
we can stay out quite late
'til a quarter past eight
and we won't wipe our feet
on the mat.
oh, it's easy to see
that i like to be me
and my pussycat likes to be him.
for we live all alone
and we do as we like,
and we like what we do
in our home.

SELF PORTRAIT

I don't iron my shirts;
I like them to match my face.

HOSPITAL ROOM

We asked them for the brightest room for Grandma.
Nothing less than private, with a view.
The quilt upon her bed was sewn with angels,
lace and little hearts, roses pink and blue.

Then, from the gallery at Eighth and Granville,
we bought several paintings bold and bright.
And everyone brought snapshots of the children
arranged them in her room in a circle of sunlight.

The church choir ladies and even the bridge club
all wrote her notes with wishes oh so kind.
With sympathy from the doctors and staff
for our dear old Grandma lame and deaf and blind.

OLD LADY IN THE SEA

An old lady lives in the sea,
her head all covered in weeds.
She'll grab at your ankles if you swim out too deep.
She'll rock you to sleep in the waves.

Children

MISCHIEVOUS TEDDY

I wish Teddy Bear would do as he's told;
although he's mischievous, I don't like to scold.
Last night he wrote crayon all over the wall.
Mommy was furious, blamed me for it all.

He tips over my milk and spills juice on the rug.
He even made Jennifer swallow a bug.
It just isn't fair that they blame it on me.
It's Teddy who's naughty. I wish they could see.

I'll have to make Teddy stand facing the wall,
and won't let him leave 'til he owns up to all.
I wish Teddy Bear would learn to be good;
not do what he shouldn't, but do what he should.

SHOPPING

when we go shopping, my mommy and me,
she buys all the groceries, like brown bread and tea
and liver and onions and, ugh! brockerly.

i grab what's important like ketchup and jam
and lic'rice and corn pops and apples and ham.
i grab crunchy-munchy and red seedless grapes
and oodles of noodles and choc'lit and dates.

i grab big buns, ice cream and sweet apple jack.
then, when we're finished, mom puts mine all back,
as i border on a tantrum attack.

A DAY AT THE ZOO

a day at the zoo;
lions, tigers, elephants too.
monkeys, penguins, long necked giraffes,
llamas, camels, hyenas that laugh.

riding a small train past rivers and lakes,
we see alligators, hippos and snakes,
zebras, leopards, birds of all kinds,
wrinkled rhinos with dusty behinds.

then, hot dogs, ice cream, candy, pop.
daddy's almost ready to drop.
baby brother's making a fuss.
it's starting to rain,
time to go home.
pack up their memories
zoo day's at an end,
but a sucker for punishment
he'll bring them again.

GHOSTLY MOON

Behind a veil of evening cloud
A ghostly moon shines down
pitching pathway back and forth
to our left, to our right,
then straight ahead,
descending streams of pearl and white
mark our journey home.

FAIRY CIRCLE

In my circle garden
Fairies dance around.
If you listen carefully you may hear
The hush and gossamer sound
Of winged dreams and ponies
Riding on their laughter

If you look closely you may see
Their majestic swirl of glitter
Visible for only a moment
As the dew falls to the ground.

NIGHT LIGHT

With fists of fury
Dark night cracks open
Spilling its molten yolk
In blazing fireworks display.
A meteor splashes down
swishing sparks into our neighbor's yard.

"How very cool!" my youngest daughter cries.
"Let's pick it up and keep it in a jar
– a night-light by my bed."

STICKY FINGER MARKS

sticky finger marks on the backs
of the dining room chairs.
Little smudges of jam
and spaghetti sauce deposits
bring a smile to my heart

Some people hate sticky finger marks
and sterile lives messed up with
peanut butter and strawberry jam.
They keep their living rooms sanitized
un-ruffled, unlived-in,
dead.

As I wipe the television screen clean
I realize how empty life would be
without my two pumpkins
scattering their seeds and fingerprints..

I love sticky finger marks...
the evidence of love.

TANTRUM TYCOON

two year old Trish has a terrible temper.
she's a tantrum tycoon when she's mad.
she can whip up a scream that's a green monster's dream.
and her face can turn blue - oh! it's bad!

last week, little Trish lay awake from a dream,
and she started to yell and she started to scream.
her tears on the floor made a puddle so deep,
dad took her sailing and rocked her to sleep.

BILLY'S BULLFROG

Billy caught a bullfrog. He kept it in a jar,
fed it flies and spiders and pet it by the hour.
He caught a garter snake down by the garden pool
and, though his dad forbade it, took both to Sunday school.

Frogs and snakes are harmless; I'm sure you'll all agree.
So Billy took them from the jar for everyone to see.
He showed the snake to Betty Jane and she let out a scream.
Next thing, two of the other girls began to make a scene.

Upstairs the congregation sang of creatures great and small
and listened to a sermon about peace on earth for all.
The pastor spoke of children, of blessings, and of joys
as piercing screams rose through the floor...heavens! what's that noise?

Billy had a bullfrog and a baby garter snake.
but taking them to Sunday school was a very sad mistake.

BILLY'S BICYCLE

watch out! watch out! everybody stand aside!
'cause here comes Billy on a bicycle ride.
he's flying along just as fast as can be.
"hey! all you people, just look at me."

straight down the sidewalk and into the park.
mom's in a dither and little dogs bark.
dad's out of breath as the bike starts to slow.
"Keep pushing, dad." Billy yells "Don't let go!"

THE WIGGLY FINGERS

when Billy's in bed and he can't get to sleep,
strange wiggly fingers tickle his feet.
it's a wiggly monster all purple and red,
and he lives in a corner right under his bed.

Billy curls up and he shuts his eyes tight,
and then he feels safe for the rest of the night.
he lies very still and he won't make a peep,
head under the covers until he's asleep.

sometimes at night when he's frightened so bad,
Billy calls for his mom and he calls for his dad.
Daddy comes in and turns on the light,
looks under the bed, not a monster in sight.

Mommy comes too and sits on his bed,
gives Billy a hug, Daddy ruffles his head.
there are no monsters here, they've all gone away,
but whoever they were, they just wanted to play

nothing can hurt you with both of us here.
we love you too much, you have nothing to fear.
Billy feels better to hear his dad speak,
he settles right down and is soon fast asleep.